Prologue

The following true story is the result of a chance encounter I had with an old college buddy about six months ago. We were talking about one of the mass shootings at the time and he told me a little bit about his friend's son. The story immediately fascinated me and I wanted to know more. He later talked to his friend and asked him if he would agree to talk to me. A month later, the three of us were having a beer in a small town bar near my friend's house. I liked Wayne (not his real name) right away. He was a dignified soft-spoken elderly man who seemed like someone I would like to get to know. After our second beer and a round of upcoming baseball season talk, I turned to Wayne and said, "Wayne, please pardon my frankness, but you just don't seem to be the type of person who could raise a mass murderer." Wayne just half smiled at me and replied, "It's a long sad story Lawrence that began many years ago." I glanced at my friend and then immediately back to Wayne, "I would like to hear more of this story if that's OK with you?" Later I found out that Wayne was just one year older than me. We, old men, were like onions of wisdom, experience, and knowledge. Our layers have been built up over many decades. It seemed like this onion would have some interesting layers to peel back and examine. Wayne, nodded his head, "Sure I have never told anyone what happened."

The next day I called Wayne on the phone and we talked for a while. He was easy to talk to and we had many things in common. It was almost refreshing to talk to him. He was at Woodstock and I was at Kickapoo Creek for the music festivals that changed the world at the time. Needless to say, that first conversation was enjoyable for both of us. As one ages, there are fewer and fewer people who are your age left alive. The chance of finding anyone you can "really" talk to becomes increasingly difficult. So as my long-dead farmer uncle would say, "We were both like pigs in shit" during that first conversation. After about 45 minutes of our best '60s stories and quite a bit of laughter, I mentioned to Wayne that I had been doing quite a bit of writing in my retirement and had recently published a book of poetry that I was extremely proud of. I told him that a series of events in the last part of my working career had led me to discovering that I could write. A reminder from Wayne's Alexa told him his doctor's appointment was scheduled in one hour. So as our conversation ended, I asked Wayne if we could talk again. Wayne's response was "Sure you can call me again Lawrence, we old hippies have to stick together".

I called Wayne the next week early in the morning. I immediately asked if it was too early to talk, to which he immediately responded "Hell no it's not too early, I have been getting up at 5:30 for over 50 years now, so by 7:30 (the time I called), I am ready to go out for a walk with the dog". "Great," I said back to him. "You know I enjoyed talking to an old Freak like you last week. It made me remember so many good times and old friends who are now gone". Using the name Freak excited Wayne and he immediately responded with, "I can't remember the last time someone called me a Freak. We were all Freaks weren't we?" A shit grin appeared on my face, "Yes, we were Wayne and some of us are still Freaks, right?" Although we were always referred to in the media as hippies, we never called each other hippies, we were always just Freaks. We were Freaks because we didn't fit in; we were the square pegs not fitting in the round holes. We were members of a counterculture that rejected almost everything about the world we were born into.

After a few minutes, I asked Wayne if he could tell me some of the things that led up to the day his son Matthew (not his real name) walked out the door of his house with a bag of guns and ammo. He said "Sure, like I said before it's a long story, but I can kind of summarize what happened in the days before he left. I have gone over everything in my mind dozens of times now. At first, it was really hard not to think about it. I still have visions of almost everything embedded in my brain. I think I have a bit of post-traumatic stress syndrome or whatever they call what soldiers go through after they come home. I am a bit afraid of things now and I don't take situations that seem 'normal' to be normal anymore. I am always 'on guard'… if you know what I mean".

About 45 minutes later in our conversation, Wayne finished telling me about the weeks leading up to "that day". At first, I didn't know what to say to him. I couldn't imagine going through what he had gone through. My first thought was "no elderly parent should have to go through something like this". Finally, as the silence at the end of his story began to feel uncomfortable, I said, "This is a story that needs to be told to the world. With your help, I think I can write this story for you and let the world know what happened. And maybe, just maybe, we can help someone like you prevent this from ever happening again."

For the next four months, Wayne and I would talk on the phone, do FaceTime and do in-person meetings, two and three times a week. Everything in the following story was created from Wayne's memories of past events and approved for publication by him.

46 years until "That Day"

Matthew (not his real name) was an adorable little boy. We discovered pretty early on that his eyes didn't seem to be right. They didn't seem to work together and they were a little crossed. So he was wearing glasses and doing therapy to correct these issues at an early age. With his blonde haircut and his wire-rim glasses, he looked like a miniature John Denver. We had just moved out of the rent-subsidized apartments we were living in and into a small older home on 15 acres of farmland in the middle of town. It was not unusual at the time for farmland that still had crops being grown on it to be in town. It had large mature trees and an Apple orchard. The rent was $215 a month. It was an ideal setting to raise Matthew and his older brother Timothy. They could run and play anywhere they wanted to. The subdivision next to the property was one of the wealthiest in town. So it was also a very safe place to live. Matthew and Timothy (not his real name) could be outside all day and we didn't worry about them at all. I worked every day at my factory job and my wife watched the kids and took care of the house. I later added a Siamese cat and a couple of bunny rabbits to the household to give the boys the experience of having animals in their lives. So I was able at the time to provide my family with a pretty idyllic life on the modest salary of a factory worker. Mathew had plenty of space and plenty of places for his "dig ups" as he called them. He loved to play in the dirt with his toy excavators and trucks. At the end of each day, I would take both of the boys down to the makeshift shower in the old basement and wash them up before bedtime. I had brought to life the Crosby, Stills, Nash, and Young song, "Our house". We were just a couple of hippies living out our dreams with our kids and our animals. Everything was good.

43 years until "That day"

I wasn't keen on public schools, so we enrolled Matthew and his brother in a private school. I didn't want my boys to be influenced by the "riffraff" of the public schools. I wanted them to have the best education and the best experience I could give them. By second grade, we seemed to have two problems with Matthew. Our first problem was with his voice. He was loud. He was very loud and didn't seem to be aware of how loud he was. He was so loud that he developed nodules on his vocal cords. We immediately put him in speech therapy and over the next three years, he learned to control the volume of his voice and the nodules disappeared. The second problem was that he didn't seem to want to do or learn anything in school. He just didn't seem to care about anything contained in books. He struggled with learning to both read and write. He just didn't want to be bothered with any of it. His mother (who was a certified teacher) tried to work with him but she always seemed to never have the time for him. She was always busy with her housework. So Mathew didn't get the help he needed from my wife.

42 years until "That Day"

Matthew's eyes seem to be getting better. The specialist tells us that his eyes don't work together. Instead of seeing one image, he sees two images. His brain is not fusing the images into one image. He tells us he does not have any depth perception. It is unlikely that he will ever be able to drive a car. My wife and I are saddened by this but his eyes seem to be working more normally. We feared that as he got older his wandering eyes would cause him to be made fun of. We continued with his eye therapy and his glasses. We hoped things would eventually get better. Mathew's elementary teacher has concerns about his lack of interest in school. He seems to only want to play and "be with his friends". His reading skills are slowly improving but he is having trouble with writing. We are not sure if his vision problems are adding to his difficulty. His teacher suggests writing exercises at home to help him. My wife makes several attempts at helping him with the exercises but quickly gives up. Matthew just puts up a stubborn resistance that she couldn't or wouldn't deal with. I am working 10 hours a day six days a week. So I had almost no time to try to work with him. It seemed that it was impossible to get him to do anything he didn't want to do.

43 years until "That Day"

This was the beginning of what would become a yearly event for Matthew and his brother Timothy. In my hometown, my dad and my brother operated a small business that allowed them the freedom in the summertime to work whenever they wanted or not at all. They owned a small property with a boat dock on the Mississippi River where they parked travel trailers. In the summertime, they spent a lot of time fishing and enjoying the outdoors next to the river. The boys of course loved the time they spent there. My mother loved having them and caring for them. Even though there were some negatives associated with the influence that my dad and brother had on them, overall it was always a good experience for the boys. It allowed time for my wife and me to be together without the work and strain of child-rearing. We were starting to have trouble getting along. My wife was beginning to be very demanding and controlling of everything associated with the house and began to go into rages when I resisted her demands or questioned her. So the time the boys were at their grandparents was helpful for our marriage and good for them.

40 years until "That Day"

Our little house on 15 acres of land was sold to a developer who wanted to put fancy homes for rich folks who were moving into town. So we were forced to move. We gave the bunnies to a friend and found a temporary home for our Siamese cat until I could get our new landlord to approve of her. Our rent was now double what we had been paying. I struggled each month to pay for it. The house was located in a student housing zone about a mile from a major university in the area. It was also about a mile from the boys' elementary school and what would become their high school. So the boys were now able to walk to and from school, in a relatively short amount of time. We no longer needed to drive them to and from school each day. Even though we were forced to leave our idyllic house with farmland, we were now close to their school and in the middle of an exciting college area. We were also within walking distance of the downtown area that had all kinds of interesting small-town stores. So it seemed like a good place for the boys to learn about the world and have positive experiences in a college town atmosphere.

39 years until "That Day"

I get a Monday morning call from the principal at Matthew's school. He is in some sort of trouble that he will tell me about when I get there. My wife was occupied working as a substitute teacher at the high school that we hoped Matthew would soon be attending. I knew the principal pretty well. As soon as I walked into his office, Alan looked up from his desk at me and said, "Thanks for coming in Wayne… a teacher caught Matthew brandishing this in the hallway today. I believe that having a butterfly knife like this is illegal in this state and it is most definitely not something a 12-year-old should be carrying around the school." I was both embarrassed and enraged by the fact that Matthew had brought something like this to school. I had no idea where he got a weapon like this or why he thought it was a good idea to bring it to school. All of the kids who attended the school were from middle-class or upper-middle-class families. It was a friendly supportive environment with kids who had above-average IQs and a desire to learn. So Matthew didn't bring the knife for protection or anything like that. I was pretty upset and punished Matthew by restricting him to home for two weeks and not allowing him to be with his friends. His friends were extremely important to him, so not being able to be with them was a severe punishment. I didn't know what else to do. I didn't want him to get kicked out of the school that I had worked so hard to get him in and keep him in. He was already struggling with almost everything in school. A change to a public school would probably be devastating for him at that point.

38 years until "That Day"

I was getting to the end of my rope with Matthew. He was falling behind in everything and failing in most subjects. He just refused to do much of anything at school. His homeroom teacher said that he only wanted to screw around with his friends and showed no interest in learning anything. I tried talking to him about the importance of learning and how it would benefit him in the future. It was like talking to the wall. He just didn't care about anything except having fun and being with his friends. We tried all sorts of punishments and motivations but nothing worked. He just didn't want to do anything associated with school or learning. I finally had my wife schedule him for a psychological evaluation at the school. The results came back indicating he was highly intelligent but had a learning disability. I was relieved by the diagnosis. I felt we just had to do what we could to help him and hopefully his intelligence would serve him well once we got him through school. From that point forward, Matthew was assigned a resource room teacher who would help him

with the subjects he was struggling with. We just had to
keep in contact with his resource teacher to track how he
was doing and what he needed to work on. It took a lot of
the pressure off of us and helped me deal with a child who
didn't want to learn.

37 years until "That Day"

Matthew followed his brother into the private high school.
We were happy that he was going to be in the high school
version of the elementary school he attended. Most of his
classmates also applied and were also admitted to the
school. So he was starting school with the same friends he
had since kindergarten. My wife had just been hired at the
same high school as a Special Education teacher. So I
breathed a sigh of relief knowing that Mathew would have
his mother literally down the hall to keep an eye on him or to
help him navigate the school system. He was assigned
another Resource Room teacher who would tutor him in
classes he was having trouble with and help monitor his
development. Mathew right away joined the football team
and his strength and size quickly made him an asset on the
defensive line. Being a football player (and a good one)
made him popular right away. Even though I had never had
any interest in the game of football, I loved going to the
games and cheering Matthew and his brother on. I was
always afraid they would be injured. But the cool air of a fall
nights and the pride of watching them both play made me
love each game I saw. They were my boys. They were
hitting hard. They were winning for their team and our
school. It just didn't get any better for a father.

35 years until "That Day"

Matthew passed his driver's education class and with the
help of a note from the eye specialist was able to obtain a

driver's license. I was still a little reluctant to let him drive the family car but he did amazingly well. He had somehow learned to see things and adapt to them despite having no depth perception at all. At least he would not be handicapped by this his entire life. I doubted that he would ever be able to back up trailers or drive large trucks, but at least he could drive a regular car. I didn't believe in buying young people cars and letting them roam the world with them, so he would have to wait until he could afford a car before he would have one. Not long after he got his license he came home one day and announced that he had quit the football team. He said he was tired of the coach telling him what to do. He had started to grow his hair a little longer and the coach told him he needed to make "himself look decent" for the team. The past hippie in me kind of understood where he was coming from but the father in me was disappointed that he was quitting. The loss of Mathew on the team was softened by the fact that his brother continued to play as a wide receiver until he graduated. I played a lot of team sports in high school and college. It seemed to help me later on in life. I always thought of any work group I was in as "our team".

34 years until "That Day"

Matthew has gotten into music in a big way. I got him a "ghetto blaster" for his birthday and he loved it. He liked some of the music from the 60s and 70s but seems to like the head-banging metal music of the day. He became a want-to-be metalhead of sorts. I didn't see anything wrong with the way he looked and dressed. My parents restricted both my hair and my clothes when I was in high school. So I was not about to restrict Matthew in the same way I was restricted. If that was the way he wanted to express his individuality, I was all for it. Since we now lived in the middle of an off-campus student area, our neighborhood was always filled with some sort of music or a party. It was sometimes hard to sleep at night during the weekends. But there was never a dull moment when the students were around. I never thought of the college students being a "bad" influence on Matthew or his brother. I don't think they ever went to any of the parties happening all around us. I was pretty strict about knowing where they were and what they were doing. I know that I would have loved to have come of age in such a fun setting. As a parent, you always try to do the best you can for your kids. I felt pretty good about the life, education, and experiences I was giving my kids.

33 years until "That Day"

At the beginning of the school year, we were forced to move again. Our landlord was selling the property to a developer who was going to build student housing on it. We finally had enough of a down payment saved up, so we finally bought a house (the same house I am still in). The house was newer and close to all the businesses and shopping in town. It was close to my work too. The location put Matthew about four miles from his last year in high school. So I bought him a junker to get him back and forth to school. It was what I called a "runabout" or it would run about a block before something broke down. But seriously, it was an OK kid's car that you really couldn't put on the highway. It worked well for getting him back and forth to school. He was having a lot of fun in his last year of school. His circle of friends seemed enormous for someone like me who had just a few friends in high school. They came over to the house all the time and spent time in Matthew's room downstairs. He had a bedroom with a bath and shower as well as a room that was his living room. There was plenty of room for kids to listen to music, watch TV or play games. His brother still had a room downstairs that he occupied when he was home from college. But for the most part, the entire downstairs belonged to Matthew.

Graduation day finally came. We were relieved that Matthew would at least have a high school diploma. What exactly he had learned during his 12 years of education was anyone's guess. I never saw him reading a book and anything that he wrote was barely legible. But he was now ready to enter the real world. Many of the kids he went to school with were off to college or other training. His best friend, Frankie (not his real name) who also needed a resource teacher in school, became best buddies and they started doing everything together. Years later Mathew told me that they grew and smoked a lot of pot and used to drink alcohol at Frankie's house.   At the time, they just seemed like kids dating girls and having a lot of fun. I was happy he was done with school and I hoped he could get into a job that he would like.

32 years until "That Day"

Matthew and Frankie both got hired by a janitorial company here in town to clean offices and restrooms. The company had one large corporate account and many other smaller business accounts in the area. The work took place in the evening once the business day was over. They were working six to seven hours a night, five days a week and sometimes on the weekend. Matthew seemed to like going to work and he liked having money in his pocket to spend. He bought himself a new stereo with a nice set of speakers. I started hearing all kinds of old and new music coming from his downstairs living room. He was still driving the car I bought him which he had affectionately named the "Chick Magnet". It was an aging and rusting Chevy Cavalier. I was happy that he had a job and was working every day but it made me sad that he was cleaning restrooms. He once told me that he had a teacher tell him, "You are not going to

amount to anything after you leave school". I thought maybe
the teacher was right and this is the best he could do. So
every day he would leave with his lunch box to pick up
Frankie in the Chick Magnet and spend the evening hours
cleaning floors and restrooms for office people. He never
complained about the work at all. Soon he was doing
special jobs like stripping and waxing floors. He soon
started describing these jobs in detail to me and how he was
able to impress the boss with his speed and efficiency. He
quickly became a trusted employee who was given the
responsibility of watching over a small crew during large
stripping and waxing jobs. I was concerned about the
chemicals he was exposed to and asked him to be careful. I
continued to hope for the best. He seemed happy and was
making money.

31 years until "That Day"

For a few months, Matthew has been coming home and
telling me about how he was doing an especially good job in
an area of their largest account. Sharp and Banes (not their
real name) was a small family business that had recently
acquired the contract to take care of all the company's
grounds maintenance. Brinkman (not their real name) was
an older company that had established a reputation for
quality and was poised to grow substantially in the future.
Matthew wanted to impress the owners with his hard work.
He said that he made sure to keep the floors, which were
littered with peanut shells, especially clean. I guess that after
a few months, he had the opportunity to talk to one of the
owners and identified himself as the cleaner who took care
of their shop. A couple more months passed with Matthew
continuing to do an extra, extra good job for the folks at
Sharp and Banes. One day he came home and announced
that they wanted to hire him for their mowing crew. So he
left the world of cleaning restrooms and started mowing

grass. He loved being outside all day and being what he called "a working man".   A couple of months later a used Ford pickup truck appeared in the driveway where the Chick Magnet used to sit. He bought it from a dealer and because he had no credit at the time, paid a criminally high-interest rate for it. I was proud that he took the initiative to get a truck on his own and didn't ask me for any help. He was now officially a "working man" with a working man's truck.

25 years until "That Day"

The six years that followed after Matthew was hired at Sharp and Banes were filled with relationships, fun, and learning. After a girl that he said he loved and wanted to marry moved away to follow a job in Chicago, he started dating a single mom with a small child. I never met the woman but he spent the best part of three years with her. He was pretty much gone for months at a time. She was always buying him nice things and she seemed like she cared about Matthew. Then one day he came home and announced that they had broken up. She wanted him to marry her and he wanted no part of marriage. I was hoping he would settle down with someone and leave home finally. After breaking up with Sue (not her real name) he started doing the party scene a lot and doing one-night stands with various women.

Matthew continued to work for the landscaping company that was growing because Brinkman was growing and building new office buildings. He was doing different kinds of jobs now when he wasn't mowing. He was planting trees and installing signs at the new properties for Brinkman. He would always come home and tell me about any "different" jobs he did that day. I was proud of everything he was doing. He struggled to sometimes get 40 hours of work in. A couple of rain days would put him in the "hours hole" and make him struggle to get an extra hour or two here or there, to try to make up for the lost time. He was making a couple of dollars above minimum wage at the time but the company provided free health insurance and had a pension plan. So I thought it was a great place for Mathew to start his working career. He was learning new things, acquiring new skills, and making money. It was all good.

20 years until "That Day"

Matthew was on again, off again living at home with my wife and me. He would live part-time with this woman or that woman. None of them seemed to last very long. I think that when the girls got serious and wanted a commitment, he decided to leave. He was becoming what we would call a "confirmed bachelor". My wife had quit her job at the school and was once again a full-time housewife. Our marriage was starting to have troubles. My wife was getting more demanding with each passing day. She seemed to have trouble getting things done in the house. She started spending a lot of time putting and keeping things in "order". She was flying into screaming rages all the time now and Matthew witnessed many of her outbursts. If I questioned anything or resisted her "orders" we would get into a massive fight. Mathew would charge out of his room and try to break up these fights. I didn't know what was happening to my wife at the time. I thought it had something to do with menopause, so I thought it all might pass. Matthew later that year traded in his used truck for a brand new Ford F-150. It was pretty exciting to have a new truck in the family. I owned a couple of trucks when I was young. He was of course as proud as a peacock of his new truck. The kid that would never "amount to anything" was working every day on a good job and had just bought a brand new truck.

18 years until "That Day"

My wife left me to live with her mother in Las Vegas. I had discovered by accident that she was suffering from a mental illness. She was spending hours "straightening" up things in the house and getting next to nothing else done as a result. This has been gradually manifesting itself over the years but once she went through menopause, the illness seemed to kick into overdrive. When I confronted her and showed her information about her illness (OCD) she denied that there was anything wrong with her. I spent the best part of a year begging her to seek some help. She refused, so I asked her to leave my house. I just refused to put up with her growing insanity. After she moved out, it was just Matthew and I left in the house. My wife had stripped the house of many decorations and furniture, so we were left with a place that felt empty and lifeless. We were still a family. I would make the dinners for us and Matthew helped around the house and yard. Timothy had moved out several years before and was settled in an apartment across town. It was a tough time for both of us, but there was finally peace in the house and this was a good thing for both of us. I felt bad that I couldn't make it work anymore. But the situation with his mother had just become intolerable. And I believed that my wife would be much happier living with her rich mother in Las Vegas. After all, her favorite things to do were drink and gamble. So Las Vegas was going to be a paradise for her.

17 years until "That Day"

Matthew spent his first time in the wilderness with a friend from work. A slightly older part-time employee at Sharp and Banes was a big-time fisherman and outdoorsman. Each year he would venture up to Minnesota, to the Boundary Waters, to fish the lakes with canoes and supplies carried by hand into the wilderness. Robert (not his real name) invited Matthew to come with him for a "real" wilderness experience. He fell in love with being miles away from civilization and people. It rekindled his love for fishing that he had as a child with my parents on the Mississippi River. He said he had a close encounter with a bear which scared the hell out of me. I guess that the presence of so many bears required special precautions to keep them away from a campsite and unable to get to the food you had. It all sounded a little too "outback" for me but he was young, fit, and strong. He got the tall German genes from my dad's side of the family and had grown to almost 6 foot 2 inches tall and weighed about 210 pounds. I was confident that he could handle himself pretty well in physically demanding situations. The next year Robert asked him to go again. This would become a yearly event over the next four years for Matthew. He would start preparing months in advance and he later started buying gear of his own to take on the trips. Before he was about to leave on the third trip he came home with a Glock 19 pistol. He had bought it locally from a gun shop and had gotten his Firearms Identification Card (FOID card) to allow him to have the weapon legally. He said that he needed something for protection in the Boundary Waters from the bears. I questioned him about the legality of having a firearm in the wilderness and he said it was common for an outdoorsman to carry a gun for protection. I was raised with firearms in the small town I grew up in. Even though I didn't currently own a firearm, I was familiar with them and I was even comfortable with them. This Glock 19 pistol was like nothing I had seen before. I put him through basic safety training on how to deal with a handgun and sent him to a friend who was going to teach him how to shoot. He loved shooting and in the years that followed he bought three more Glock handguns and a 22 rifle. Where I came from, everyone owned a gun. When we were kids, we would shoot our rifles and occasionally a shotgun in the front yard of the house. So I didn't see anything wrong with gun ownership or shooting.

15 years until "That Day"

Mathew continues to work at Sharp and Banes. He has become a respected veteran who can do all kinds of jobs for the company including operating a Bob Cat for both dirt and snow removal. His childhood fascination and dream with the "dig ups" had turned into reality. He loves operating heavy equipment. During the mowing season, he is a working supervisor of a large mowing crew. He consistently does high-quality work and is always praised by the owners for this work. Some of the older original members of the crew have started to retire. He tells me about guys that helped him learn this or learn that. They are hiring younger people, some of which Mathew begins to train and mentor. He is becoming someone who is looked up to. He has "been there and done that" before some of the new guys were out of grade school. He begins to come home with stories about the company's mechanic who is always giving him shit. He is best friends with one of the owners so he seems to be able to do and say anything he wants without fear of discipline.   He is constantly making fun of Mathew and routinely blames him for equipment problems he had nothing to do with. Most of the time Mathew just ignores him but occasionally they get into heated arguments. Bob (not his real name) seems like a pompous asshole who needs his teeth rearranged. The owners are aware of the abuse Bob is giving Mathew (and other employees) but refuse to do anything about it. This seems to get under Mathew's skin. I just tell him to ignore the guy since he is just a mechanic and not a boss of any kind. I just hope the owners will discipline or fire this guy.

14 years until "That Day"

Mathew has started smoking cigarettes and going to the local bars. He has become an after-hours "working man" now. He is hanging out with a lot of the local tradesmen that head to taverns after work for a cold one or many cold ones, after a day of working their asses off in the hot sun or the cold winter. He tells me about the tradespeople that he knows. Dry Wallers and Painters are all alcoholics. Ironworkers are badasses who could drink you under the table and then kick your ass if you step out of line. So he begins to come home a couple of nights a week after having a "few beers". His brother had recently wrecked his car (that I bought for him) and was charged with driving under the influence of alcohol. So I was always telling him to call me or get a cab or walk if he had too much to drink. It was always "Don't worry Dad, I got this". Losing his license would mean he really couldn't do his job anymore. The kid that had no depth perception had to tow and back up large trailers of equipment and machines. He needed to have his wits about him to do this. I was concerned about the drinking he was doing. His mother drank almost every day and his brother was now attending AA meetings. The hereditary nature of alcoholism is pretty well accepted. So I hoped that Mathew was not slipping into becoming an alcoholic. I pretty much hated alcohol and didn't drink at all. I smoked a lot of pot during the 60s and had a couple of LSD experiences. Once I had kids, the penalties associated with possession made it impossible for me to continue using drugs. I didn't want my ability to provide for my family to be ruined by my selfish desire to get high.

7 years until "That Day"

I decided to retire from my job at age 62. I wanted to do some things before I got too old. I had a small business that I wanted to start and I had a burning desire to learn how to play the piano. Retirement would give me the freedom that I needed to finally do the things I wanted to do. So I threw myself into retirement with an intensity that is usually reserved for your first job. I was working more hours than during my regular job but enjoying it a hell of a lot more. In my free time, I was practicing piano and learning to read music. I was having a great time. Mathew was also having the success that I never dreamed he would have. He was given a salaried position at Sharp and Banes. His salary, bonuses, and fringe benefits were excellent. At this point, I thought he should start giving me some room and board money. I had always made good money and never asked him to contribute to the bills. Now that his salary exceeded what I was making, I thought he should start giving me some money. What I asked for just covered the extra utility expenses I incurred with him living with me. So I didn't ask for a lot of money. He seemed OK with what I was asking for and started paying me the amount each month.

6 years until "That Day"

Mathew going on salary seems like it was a bad idea now. He doesn't have that go-get-the-hours attitude he had before. Now he gets paid no matter what he does or doesn't do. He is not getting up to get to work on time anymore. I am Mr. Time. I am rarely late to anything and will always arrive at any appointment or work 15 or 20 minutes ahead of time. So as you might imagine, this does not set with me very well. My normal time to get up is around 5:30 AM. I have been doing this for 50-plus years. So when it is 6:30 AM and I don't hear any movement downstairs, I start to get anxious. My anxiety soon gets the best of me and then I go downstairs and knock on his door. "Are you going to work today?" I ask through the door. The answer is "Yaa…I'm getting up now". Looking at my watch tells me that unless he flies out of the bed like a banshee from hell, he is going to be late. It seems that getting to work on time now is optional for him. This of course drives Mr. Time insane. I worked 11 years on my last job and was never late once. I missed only two days of work because of an abscessed tooth. So I am wired to honor my commitments to the people I work for. It's just the way I am. I have almost no respect for people who are habitually late. Before Mathew was salaried he would be on time because being late would cost him money. Now the salary man didn't care. He got paid no matter what time he decided to drag his ass into work. This was disgusting to me.

4 years until "That Day"

Mathew's once-new truck is looking like it is needing to be replaced. It's turning into a rust bucket and it has numerous problems that would be expensive to fix. It's not my business to ask if it is going to be replaced, so I just continue to hope that one day I will see a different truck parked in the driveway. I am concerned about what is happening to all of Mathew's money. He is not buying anything but he seems to not have any money. He is not paying his room and board payment on time anymore. I am having to ask him for it. He gives me excuses like he will give me the money next week. He is having some sort of money problems. I don't ask what is going on. He is making around $60,000 a year and besides what he pays me and his cell phone, he has no other payments that I know of. I am starting to think that he has some sort of debt to pay that I don't know about. I imagine he has some gambling debt or child support to some woman he might have impregnated in the past. He wouldn't tell me if I asked him or he would not tell me the truth. I realized many years ago that he tells me (and others) exactly what they want to hear. He is an expert at manipulating people. He is spending a lot more nights at the bar and thankfully not driving when he does. I hear him come home late many nights. I can sometimes hear him stumble as he walks through the foyer and to the stairs leading downstairs. He is shitfaced drunk.

Mathew is beginning to be the old timer at work as all the older guys retire. His original boss, the Operations Manager is preparing to retire in a few years. The owners have handed the management of the company to one of the owners' sons and a cousin. Mathew doesn't like either one of them. They want to make changes in the way things are done. Mathew says they are entitled "rich pricks" who have never worked an entire day in their lives. He is still having trouble with Bob the mechanic. Mathew tells me they get into shouting matches now. I tell him to just walk away but Mathew says he refuses to back down. This guy sounds like a real bully. The management just refuses to do anything about his behavior. I find it hard to believe he is allowed to treat employees this way.

1 & 1/2 years until "That Day"

A different truck appeared in the driveway right before Christmas. It was not a new truck. It was an older truck. It was the same color as Mathew's old truck, sporting some rust and looking very "used". His other truck was still parked in the same spot it had been for the last four months, in the parking lot at work. It had died one day and Mathew borrowed a work truck for transportation. When I asked him about it, he said he bought it from a relative of one of the owners who works at Sharp and Banes. He paid $5000 for it from the $5000 Christmas bonus he had just received. I was glad he didn't have any payments but it seemed that he had spent $5000 to get a little bit better pile of junk than he had before. He didn't bother to show me the truck or take me for a ride in it. I asked him how mechanically sound it was and he told me, "It's good enough to get me by for a while". I thought that considering the money he was making, there should be a brand-new truck sitting in the driveway. I didn't know what his credit was like. He had a couple of credit cards that sent bills each month. I thought maybe he didn't qualify for a loan. He had not been able to save any money since he had to use all of his Christmas bonus to buy this truck. It seemed strange considering all the money he was making. I am still barely getting his room and board money. It was starting to be a monthly pain in the ass for me. I didn't want to be bugging him for money all the time. He was always gone or busy or sleeping, so it was hard for me to catch him. This began to be a monthly thing I had to go through.   I began to wonder if he owed money to the mob or had a large gambling debt. He had played the lottery for years and was always talking about what he would do when he wins "the big one". He is spending more nights now at his favorite bar. He is starting to use Uber to take him there in the late afternoon and return him later that night. Uber makes it easier for him to drink and drink a lot. Besides the weekend, he added two and three nights of drinking to his schedule. I had no idea how much money he is spending drinking this many days a week, but it has to be a lot. Being someone who didn't drink and was always very good with money, I just could not understand how anyone could throw money away like this. At first, he would tell me he was just going for the social aspect of the bar scene. He knew I thought it was a horrible place to spend time. He had been from little on, a very social person. He always seemed to have dozens of friends and was always doing or going somewhere with them. But lately, it has turned into "I am going to have a couple of beers with my friends". It was starting to seem like all his friends now are "drinking" friends.

1 year until "That Day"

It's now August of 2021 after all the Covid 19 lockdown business had started to wind down. Mathew had spent the lockdown with a woman who lives in a local trailer court a few miles from here. Every few weeks he would show up at the house to get something and tell me what he was up to. Like most of his women, he didn't tell me her full name and I had no idea what she looked like. She worked as a cook at a school cafeteria. Janet (not her real name) likes to drink. So they shared a love of the bottle. One evening he suddenly shows up at the house with all the belongings he had gradually taken over to Janet's house. Mathew's story is that she got shit-faced drunk and they got into a big fight. He tells me that one of her favorite things to do was drink and fight. So Mathew is officially done living with her. I was disappointed because I thought he had finally found someone who he could live with and would finally leave my house. So he is back living with me again. Most of the bars were closed so he was not going out but he is working every day. Pot had just become legal in our state, so he enthusiastically started buying and smoking a lot of weed. I am amazed at the amount of weed he is buying and smoking. I still think it is better than booze. To me, except for hard drugs, anything is better than booze.

9 months until "That Day"

The Operations Manager, John (not his real name) who had been Mathew's boss since he started has retired. Mathew had in so many words (for several years) told me he was the heir apparent and would assume his position when he retired. The new management has changed the equation by openly declaring they wanted to get rid of the less adaptable older employees and replace them with younger more "progressive" people. John and Mathew were the only two older employees left. The new management had been grooming a new younger guy to replace John when he decided to retire. Mathew tells me has essentially been John's right-hand man for years and knows the job very well. But he is not a "yes" man and this disqualifies him for the position. Mathew refers to all of the lower-level managers they have recently hired as "dick suckers" who will do whatever they are asked, no matter how wrong or stupid it is. John has been protecting Mathew from the insane demands of the two new managers. So while the rest of the company begins to change into a dysfunctional parody of its former self, Mathew continues to work and do the same things, the same way he had done them for almost 30 years, with John going to bat for him when the new management tried to interfere. Now that John is gone, Mathew has no one left to protect him and he is now being ordered around by a couple of "dumb ass kids" (his words).

6 months until "That Day"

Mathew came home from work enraged about his Christmas bonus. The $5000 bonus from last year turned into a $1000 bonus this year. "I was counting on that money, I have people I need to pay," he tells me. He says that he made a major contribution to the profitability of the company and deserves more money. He said they are just screwing him and trying to demoralize him (my words here), so he will quit. He is also fighting again with Bob the mechanic and the situations sound like they are close to an actual fistfight. Mathew has been at the bar a lot and tells me that he is pretty much high all day at work. He is vaping pot oil all the time. I don't know how much he is spending but it must be a lot. I gave up asking him for any room and board money, a couple of months ago. I just got tired of the constant excuses and run around he gives me. I finally said to myself, "Fuck it, I can't take this anymore". I don't know what the hell is going on with him. He is continually late for work anymore. I have given up going down to his room to wake him up. I look at the clock next to my bed and see that he is leaving when he should be arriving at his work. This drives "Mr. Time" nuts of course. I can't fathom being late to work or making being late a regular occurrence. Then I go down to his living room area to put something in there and I find a god-awful mess. I rarely go down there for anything. I am not the type of person to invade someone else's privacy. But when I walked into the room, I was greeted by a room floor filled with trash and empty soda cups from the Hucks gas station up the street. It looked like the start of a landfill. My first thought was "This is going to attract roaches". He had stopped taking the trash out of his room. I had no idea where Mathew was or when I would see him again, so got four large garbage bags and filled them up with the trash that was everywhere. I didn't get all the trash but I got most of it. He came back home a couple of days later and didn't say anything to me about the missing trash. So I didn't say anything to him, but he continued to accumulate trash for reasons I didn't understand. A week later there was more trash and more empty Hucks cups. His room was now a landfill.

5 months until "That Day"

It's Mathew's favorite time of year, winter. He loves to plow snow with the big equipment that Sharp and Banes use. He had become the company's best operator. His childhood fascination with the "dig ups" has become reality for him. We have already had a couple of big snows that required him to be out for many hours at a time. He tells me he can go 36 hours without sleep and continue to work. This seems impossible to me but he can do it with ease. I would be hallucinating and falling asleep after 15 hours of work. I don't know how (or why) he does this. Few people have fun at their jobs, but when he is plowing snow he is in heaven.

He came home with the news that he had found God and had been going to a local church. He had wanted to tell me earlier I think but might have been afraid of my reaction. I have not been very enthusiastic about organized religion for a long time. I never discouraged anyone in my family from going to church or believing in God. It was always with me, "Whatever gets you through the night is alright as long as no humans or animals are hurt". I have always been a very spiritual person and I had gone to church regularly in my younger days. About 40 years ago, I began studying the world's religions in search of one I would like. I didn't find a religion but I did find a philosophy that has guided me for most of my life now. I am a follower of the Tao or a Taoist. So I was somewhat relieved and happy that Mathew had found the lord and was going to church. He was also "serving" several times a week at the church during the week. "Serving" was working around the church doing set-ups for functions or cleaning up after functions. He tried to get me to meet his pastor and attend a service but I respectfully decline his offer. I am happy that Mathew appears to be changing his life. I hope he would meet a nice girl at church that he could eventually marry. I thought his lifetime of being a partier and playboy had finally come to an end.

Two weeks before he revealed that he had found the lord, I noticed that he seemed to have lost weight. He was getting very thin. Out of concern that he had something horrible, I asked him about it. He said that he had just stopped drinking all the soda pop that he had been drinking. He is also starting to go on long walks in the middle of the night and is lifting weights in the basement workout area that we still have. I am of course pleased that he is working out and turning his life of debauchery around. I later find out that he has a crush on a 25-year-old part-time bartender at his favorite bar. She is young and beautiful. He says that "I want to marry this girl". The girl is about one-half his age making this all seem a bit unrealistic. But I am happy he seems to be changing his life in so many positive ways. I am still hoping for a nice older church girl to appear and drag him to the altar.

4 months until "That Day"

Mathew is still plowing the snow that occasionally falls on our area. But since he is salaried he still needs to go in every day and hang around in case something needs to be done. Most of the time he tells me he goes out to police the grounds (pick up trash) and ends up driving around all day smoking pot. He comes in with a bag from the dispensary several times a week. Sometimes he would come home after work and ask me "Guess how many hours I worked today?" And I would say a low number of hours to which he would reply, "I worked a total of 20 minutes and I am kind of proud of myself". The management was starting to get on him again about being late. I told him that he was poking the bear by being late all the time. He said he didn't give a shit about what they thought. He worked extra hours all the time, so it shouldn't matter if he is five or ten minutes late. He is still getting into pissing matches with Bob the mechanic. I just hope they don't come to blows. Bob is best friends with one of the owners and would probably keep his job and Mathew would probably get fired.

16 weeks until "That Day"

Mathew and Bob the mechanic got into a major fight at work. It was a major screaming match with Mathew telling me he was screaming at the top of his lungs at Bob while one of the new managers sat in an office not far away. The incident was so upsetting that Mathew called his new operations manager later and asked if he could take the following week off to try to get over what had just happened. His new boss told him he was free to use the vacation days he still had remaining if he liked. It sounded like someone should have

intervened, but I guess no one did. I told him to just spend
the week serving at church, getting in shape, and thinking
about getting a new job somewhere. I could easily put
together a resume for him and with his skills and experience,
I was sure he could easily get a new job here in town
quickly. I just wished the management would do something
about this Bob guy. He has been a thorn in Mathew's ass for
years and now things are getting dangerously serious.

15 weeks until "That Day"

Just one month shy of working 30 years for Sharp and
Banes, Mathew was fired. They gave him a check for $2500
and sent him out the door. Mathew said he didn't get any
termination paperwork or a solid reason for his termination
other than "We have had enough of you" from the guy who
fired him. This of course didn't seem right in any way and it
even sounded illegal. Mathew was happy it happened and
said that they played right into his hand. He believed that
they had spent the last six months doing discriminatory
things to try to force him to quit. He had been collecting
evidence in the form of text messages and eyewitness
accounts from trusted coworkers. Now he was going to sue
them and take their company away from them. He was off to
schedule a retirement party at his favorite bar and try to get
his 25-year-old heartthrob to be the bartender. The best
thing had just happened to him. He was out of Sharp and
Banes and he was going to be rich.

13 weeks until "That Day"

It has been two solid weeks with Mathew talking about the
details of the lawsuit he is going to file. He shows me text
messages and tells me stories that weave a narrative of
abuse and discrimination. The owner of his favorite bar has
a daughter who is a big-time lawyer, I guess. Mathew is

going to ask the bar owner to ask his daughter to recommend an attorney for him. I knew from my experience of helping a friend with an employment lawsuit that it is difficult to find attorneys who will take these cases. So I was happy he was going to use his connections to get a good attorney to pursue this case. He constantly talked about how much money he was going to get and what he was going to do with it. They had played right into the 11D chess (his words) that he was playing. Now all their money and their company were going to be his. What he showed me seemed to show discrimination, but I knew that he would have to put together a solid narrative with evidence to win a case like this. I encouraged him to file for unemployment compensation so he wouldn't be immediately forced to find a new job. He didn't want to file for some reason. He says, "Just lazy fucks and slackers do the unemployment thing". A couple of days later he tells me he is going to cash out his 401K. The company had recently converted its pension plan into a 401K. All the money in it was an employer contribution. He had never put a dime in it. I told him it would make sense to take a little out to get him by for a while and roll most of it into another 401K or an IRA. I thought he could live on some of it until he could get the lawsuit done. No, he was going to cash it all out now.

11 weeks until "That Day"

Mathew came home with a $110,000 check made out to him. He had cashed in his 401K. He has me take a picture of it with my phone. I ask him if he had talked to the owner of the bar about the attorney for the lawsuit. He said he had not "had a chance to talk to him yet but would soon". He said he didn't like going in there much anymore because the bitches in there were always calling him a dirty old man or a pedo for hitting on the 25-year-old bartender.   A few minutes later he was off to his bank to deposit his retirement money into his account. At this point, I decided to contact an attorney that I knew and went to college with years ago. I knew he was retired but he would know someone who could help us with this. Mathew's literacy was a bit of a handicap in this type of situation. As a retired bureaucrat, I was pretty sure I could prepare any documentation Mathew would need for the lawsuit. It would be a piece of cake for me and I looked forward to working on it. If my boy had been wronged and discriminated against, I would do whatever I could to help him seek justice and win compensation.

10 weeks until "That Day"

Mathew appears to be happy and enjoying himself. He has bought some fancy clothes. He no longer wears his jeans and t-shirt outfits that I was accustomed to seeing on him. He is wearing good clothes all the time now. The working man is now apparently gone. Mathew was continuing to serve at the church one day a week. He talked about doing other volunteer work in the community. He knew that I had spent many years volunteering my time to help my community. I told him that he was a natural for Habitat for Humanity. I knew the guy in charge of building the houses for the disadvantaged and offered to give him a call and set Mathew up with an interview. He still had not had a chance to investigate the attorney for his upcoming lawsuit. I showed him the biographical information of the attorney my friend had recommended. She was an employment law attorney who specialized in wrongful termination cases. He said he would give her a call tomorrow. I immediately offered to help him prepare the narrative and evidence to present to the attorney. He responded with, "I got this Dad, I got everything I need to get millions from these guys."

8 weeks until "That Day"

Mathew has gotten into a routine of staying up half the night, getting up, smoking weed, watching TV, and sitting on the porch. Occasionally he will make himself something simple to eat but most of the time he goes somewhere to get carry-out food. He has been eating carry-out food and pizzas for years now. I am too busy to make big meals anymore. He is rarely around when I do cook "a meal". My business partner will cook for me several times a week and occasionally we go out to a local restaurant.

Mathew is only going to the bar once a week now. He hasn't stopped drinking but he has cut back quite a bit. He seems to not be on his phone very much anymore. A lot of his friends were work friends so he doesn't talk to them anymore. He was always texting and on the phone with all his friends and coworkers. Now he just sits on the porch most of the day without his phone or his iPad. There is no mention of the lawsuit anymore or talk about what he is going to do with all the money. All of that seems to be gone completely. I don't say anything to him about it anymore. I don't understand why he does not want to move forward with the lawsuit. When I mention getting even a part-time job, so he won't deplete his retirement money he says, "I will be making big money when the snow starts falling and companies need operators". So I guess he is going to sit on his ass until it snows.

4 weeks until "That Day"

The weather has turned really hot. Mathew seems to be obsessed with how cool I am keeping the house. If it is not too warm, I will open up the house in the evening and put fans in the windows to bring in the night air. I love the night air and pretty much hate the air conditioning. He seems to regularly come upstairs to check the temperature on the digital thermometer that I have in the kitchen. He is constantly asking me to turn the air conditioning down because of the heat. I set it where I have set it for 20 years and I am not enthusiastic about a higher electric bill because "it's really warm downstairs" for him. He then asks me with this preface "I hope you don't think I'm crazy" and then proceeded to tell me how he brought the trash bin back to the house. He thinks I always put it out too early and "it looks tacky out there". I guess (in his mind) I should wait until the cover of darkness to put the trash bin to the road. I have been putting the trash out to the road like this for decades and now this is a problem for him. Anyway, I said OK and he later wheeled the trash bin out to the road after it got dark.

He continues to lose weight and is starting to look like he just came out of a concentration camp.   I still see him bringing huge cups of Hucks soda into the house. He is losing weight because he is not eating. He used to be a pretty good-looking guy. Now his facial features are sharp and drawn making him look like a caricature of his former self. His new clothes seem to fit him but I doubt any of his old clothes would. I think he may have lost 50 pounds. It's like he is a different person now. The only thing that he is doing outside the house is his weekly "serving" at church. He goes for maybe three hours and comes back home. He is doing nothing else. I am amazed at exactly how little he is doing. He is doing nothing to help me at the house. I thought he might get the mower out and mow the lawn but he said he was done with mowing grass. I am doing more in the first four hours of each day than he does in an entire week. This is amazing to me and I am starting to be concerned about him.

2 weeks until "That Day"

It was still hot outside. Mathew is continuing his routine of basically doing nothing. A couple of months ago, I bought one of those Amazon Blink cameras to be able to check up on my dog when I was gone. I never activated the service to be able to set it up for motion detection. It was three dollars a month for the service, so I decided to finally sign up and activate the camera. I am gone for a few hours every day with my business and with other things I do. I wanted to see what Mathew was up to when I was gone. I didn't tell him that the camera was now able to activate and record the activity of anyone in the room. The first day I activated it, I got numerous activation recordings of Mathew coming upstairs to check the temperature in the house. He came up to check it five times in just one hour. He was obsessed with the temperature in the house for some reason. Now I am getting concerned about what is happening to my son. I decided to look online for the causes of having no ambition to do anything. It turns out this is called avolition. It is defined as "the lack of motivation or inability to undertake an activity or task with an end goal, such as attending school or completing chores. In most cases, medical experts associate avolition with schizophrenia, bipolar disorder, severe depression, or a side effect of medications". After a quick search of the illness associated with avolition, it was pretty obvious that Mathew was suffering from a bipolar disorder. In the mania phase listed on the Mayo Clinic's website, he had eight out of eight symptoms. In the depressive phase, he had seven out of nine symptoms. My son had a severe mental illness that was transforming him into someone different.

1 week until "That Day"

All week Mathew was staying at a local hotel in a room. He tells me a friend from out of town had booked it and wasn't using it. I know the hotel and it is about two miles away from

my house. It's a nice place to stay. So I think, "That's good
for him, he can turn the air conditioning to a polar setting and
be happy for a few days". After three days he pops into the
house and says there is someone in the hotel who he thinks
is watching who comes and goes with the intent of breaking
into their rooms and robbing them. This guy is in the room
next to him and Mathew is planning some sort of sting
operation to catch him. He tells me he is even banging a
drawer when he comes back to the room to make the robber
think he is putting a gun in it. All of this is told to me as he is
gathering more stuff to take to the hotel room. When he is
about to leave he says, "Do yourself a favor Dad, and crank
that air conditioning down, there is a windfall coming your
way".

3 days until "That Day"

I sent Mathew a text to see how he was doing. I was a bit
worried that he had gotten into the middle of some kind of
criminal activity. I didn't know what was going on but I didn't
want him to get hurt by some mob guy or crazy criminal. I
get no reply to my text. I could always text Mathew any time
of day or night and he would reply very quickly. I sent
another text a couple of hours later. No reply to that text
either. I go to bed and decide to call him in the morning. I
call him at about 9 AM the next day. The phone rings and it
goes to voicemail. I proceed to text and call him multiple
times the entire day. He doesn't return my calls or text
messages. I am starting to get worried about him. Is he
lying dead in a ditch somewhere because he got in the
middle of some organized robbery operation? I don't know
what to do. I even drove to the hotel to see if I can spot his
truck in the parking lot. When I get to the hotel, I can't find
his truck anywhere in the parking lot. I want to call the
police, but what do I tell them? Things are starting to get a
bit crazy.

1 day until "That Day"

I had just gotten back to the house in the morning when I get a call from Enterprise Rent-a-Car. The young man on the other end of the line was trying to contact Mathew. He tells me that the car he dropped off late last night was damaged and he had left his debit card in it. Why they had my number, I didn't know. I told the young man that I would tell him that he called. This of course nearly made me lose my mind. Why was he renting a car? Where was his truck? Was his truck broken down? What the hell is going on here? I can't reach him and now he doesn't have a debit card. This really upset me. I continued most of the day trying to call him. His phone would ring and then go to voicemail. It was obvious that Mathew did not have his phone with him.

10 hours until "That Day"

Suddenly Mathew comes in the door at about 8 p.m. I am relieved to see him. I immediately tell him about Enterprise calling and what they said. I asked what was going on. I told him I was worried sick about him. I told him I thought something bad had happened because of the hotel thief he was trying to entrap. "No that turned out to be nothing and I'm Ok. I will tell you all about it in the morning" he explains as he goes out the door with a sleeping bag in his hand. I figure he is going to sleep at someone's house now and needs a sleeping bag. I am relieved that he is back and I won't need to identify his body.

"That Day"

It's 6:00 in the morning. I am at my computer in the dining room checking my e-mail and creating an invoice to send to one of our customers. When I look over my computer monitor I can look through the sliding glass door that leads to the elevated deck on my house. It's a nice scene with the deck and all the mature trees and bushes surrounding it. I can watch the weather and squirrels from where I sit with just a glance over my computer screen. Suddenly a uniformed police officer is standing in front of the sliding glass door. He sees me sitting there and knocks on the door. I immediately go to the door and open it. "Hello sir, we got a call from your neighbor that someone is sleeping in your backyard. I just need to know if it is alright for this guy to sleep in your yard?" With what had to have been a shocked look on my face "Someone is sleeping in the yard? I didn't know anyone was sleeping back here?" At this point Mathew yells up at both of us, "It's me down here, Dad" with a disgusted tone to his voice. I turn to the police officer and told him that he is my son and it was OK. The officer apologizes for the inconvenience and leaves. "Why are you sleeping in the backyard"? I ask him in a voice that will carry to where he is laying in the grass under a bush. He responds with "I like the night air".

Soon he comes into the house with the sleeping bag in his hand. I go out the front door as he is coming in. I notice his truck is not there. I ask him where his truck is. "It's over at the hotel" he replies. "Do you need a ride to pick it up?" I ask him. He heads down to his room telling me someone is coming over to take him to his truck. "So when are they coming over and how do they know to come over here if you don't have your phone?" I ask him. He yells up the stairs at me "They know I am here, Dad. They will be here in a few minutes". He is back out on the porch now in his usual chair. I ask him again when this person is going to take him to his truck. "They are coming at 1 o'clock. I am going to take a nap now" as he heads downstairs to his room. He just got out of his sleeping bag less than 40 minutes before from sleeping all night in the back yard and now he needs a nap.

At this point, I need to leave to check on my business, so I go downstairs to his room door and tell him I am leaving and I can easily drop him off at his truck. He says no he wants to take a nap. Talking through the door I tell him "I can easily drop you off Mathew, it's no problem for me. I don't understand why you don't want me to take you to your truck? What is going on here?" Within five seconds the door to his room flew open and he charged out at me with a look on his face that I had never seen before. There was anger and hate, unlike anything I had ever seen in anyone before. I thought he was going to hit me as he got right in my face and screamed "I'm a grown-ass man and I can do what I want, so let ME alone". This completely freaked me out. So I just backed off and said "OK, Ok I was just trying to help, I'm taking off now." Even though he had lost weight he was still much bigger than me. With my advanced age of 72, one punch from him could kill or cripple me. Now, I am afraid of him.

40 minutes after my arrival at my business, my phone starts to notify me that Mathew is upstairs doing something. I check the first three video clips. He is checking the temperature again. Then I check the fourth clip. Mathew is now dressed in an old faded button-down short-sleeved shirt that hung on him like he had just been released from Dachau and an old ball cap that I had never seen before. The guy who was dressed all the time like a famous actor now looked like he was auditioning to be a homeless person in a movie. In the video clip, he walked up to my dining room table and laid one of his 9mm Glocks down on it. He then proceeded to load a magazine with bullets. I had not seen any of his guns in at least ten years. If fact, we had a discussion a couple of months before about how he needed to renew his long-expired Firearms Identification Card. Watching him with one of his guns now and watching him

load up a magazine scared the shit out of me. I thought I would come home and be greeted by hot lead.

I did the only thing I could do. I called the police. I told them I would meet them at my house in ten minutes. Ten minutes later four squad cars met me on the street just up from my house and out of sight. I told them what had happened and I was afraid he was going to shoot me. With guns drawn, four officers were going to surround the house and two officers were going to knock on the door and try to get Mathew to come out. It was like a scene out of a movie. At this point, some of my neighbors were outside wondering what was going on. The police directed me to a safe distance, so I couldn't really see what was going on. I hoped that Mathew wouldn't do anything stupid and get himself killed by the police. I was also afraid one of the officers would get shot and lose his life. This was a full-fledged nightmare now.

It all was happening so fast that I felt like I was in a bad dream. The sergeant who I talked to when I arrived came over to talk to me again. He said that as the two officers approached the front door, Mathew was just coming out with a duffel bag full of guns and ammo. Just then an ambulance rolled up and I could see Mathew being escorted into it. Since he didn't have a Firearms Identification Card, they confiscated all the guns he had in the duffel bag and suggested that he go to the hospital for an evaluation. They could have arrested him for illegal possession of firearms and Mathew knew it. So going to the hospital was a much better deal than jail. The sergeant asked me for permission to search and clear my house of any additional firearms. I gave them permission and I assisted the two officers in searching my house. We found two more guns and quite a bit of ammunition. The police took the guns and allowed me to take the ammunition to a friend's house. So I loaded up the boxes of ammo in my car and took it across town.

As I am loading up the ammunition, the sergeant comes over to my car. He tells me I need to go to the hospital after I secure the ammunition to talk to the doctors who will be examining Mathew. It takes me about 40 minutes to arrive at the hospital. I go in and inform the receptionist who I am and why I am there. She tells me to have a seat and that the doctor would be talking to me in a few minutes. I have been seated for maybe five minutes and Mathew walks in a sits down next to me. He has a piece of paper in his hand and tells me he is ready to go. He smiles and tells me, "Don't worry Dad, God still loves you". I looked directly at him and immediately responded with a stern, "I don't think we should be talking right now". Suddenly a young female doctor walks up and asks me to follow her. When she closes the door to a small examination room, I immediately ask her what the hell is going on. She said she had talked to him and decided to release him. At this point, I am in disbelief that they have discharged him this quickly. I tell her about what had just happened and why he was there. Her eyes got wider as I talked about him leaving my house with a duffle bag of guns and ammo that he was not licensed to have. She finally asks me if I believed he was a danger to himself or others. To which I said, "Yes, I think he was going to kill everyone at his former employer and then commit suicide by cop." At this point, the doctor realizes that she had been completely buffaloed by Mathew and she had made a grievous error in judgment. She heads for the door and as she opens it says, "Just stay here, I am going to have a nurse get him back in here for a psychological evaluation". I left a few minutes later and went home. This was the worst day of my life.

I decided I had to tell his brother what happened. This was not something I could wait until he was off of work. It had to be done now. I needed to talk to someone. After I pulled into the parking lot of his work, I got a call from the sergeant who wanted to know what was happening with Mathew. I proceeded to tell him that they had released him and that I had intervened in time to get him a psychological evaluation. The sergeant was pretty upset that they had just decided to quickly release him. He wanted to know the name of the doctor who made the decision. He then thanked me for doing the right thing. I ended the conversation with, "I have always tried to do the right thing all my life, sergeant. Thank you and your men for your service today."

After pulling Timothy out of his work to tell him what had just happened, I drove home. My son was now in the hospital being evaluated by professionals. I believed that my intervention had probably saved the lives of many people and probably saved his life too. Now Mathew was going to get the help he so desperately needed. I thought there was no need to call the hospital right away to check on his status. I would call the next day and see what was going on with my son.

1 day after "That day"

At noon the next day, I called the hospital to check on Mathew. They gave me a number for a mental health organization here in town that handles things like this. The girl on the other end of the line couldn't tell me any details about Mathew other than he was transported to a mental hospital in St Louis, Missouri. She gave me the name of the hospital and when he was admitted. She told me to call the hospital tomorrow for more information about his treatment. It was of course horrible to have your son admitted to a mental hospital but I felt relieved. I didn't know if our hospital here could deal with someone with a severe mental illness. So I was thankful that he was going to a place where he could get the help he needed. I just wanted him to get better.

2 days after "That Day"

At 10 a.m. the next day, I called the mental hospital in St Louis. They refused to divulge any information about him to me. The young man I talked to said that if he was in the hospital, he would have signed a form giving me the right to know about his status. So in so many words, he told me (without really telling me) that Mathew had not given permission for me to know anything about what was happening to him. He had shut me out. There was little I could do now. I just had to wait and hope that the hospital would treat him and help him get started on the road to recovery.

6 days after "That Day"

Early in the afternoon, I get a call from the police department. They tell me Mathew was found in a ditch on the side of the road about 70 miles from here. He was alive but severely dehydrated and had been walking a long distance. They said he was in the hospital and wanted to come home.

When I got to the hospital and walked into his room he was eating a large hamburger and a plate of fries. He looked like hell. His clothes were dirty and ripped in several places. He was extremely thin and looked like he had walked through a desert. He was happy to see me and just wanted to go home.

He proceeds to tell me that they kept him for three days and then released him. They gave him a bus token to get to the train station. He decided to just start walking in the direction of home instead. This is a distance of over 350 miles, so I am amazed that he was able to get as far as he did. He said the hospital was a filthy prison and he had a roommate with a horrible disease of some sort. He had some release paperwork that was folded and torn with a number for someone here he was supposed to call for counseling when he got back.

Has he was getting ready to leave with me, I stepped out of the room and tried to get someone to talk to me about what kind of treatment (if any) he got. No one knew anything other than he had someone to call and set up an appointment with. At this point, it appeared that he had been warehoused for three days and sent on his way. I didn't know what to do. I had to take my son home.

We get home and he gets a shower. He gets some clean clothes on and goes to sleep in his room. A couple of hours later he wakes up. He needs cigarettes. He still has no debit card, so I drive to the gas station to get him a pack of cigarettes. When I get back, he is in the kitchen eating some chips and salsa that I had put out for him. Out of the blue, he says, "Yeah, I was in a bad place….I had been thinking about what they did to me for months now". I ask him about where his truck was. He had it towed from the hotel by a friend who has a towing service. It has been sitting in the guy's business lot ever since. He left his cell phone in it and Enterprise Rent-a-Car still has his debit card.

A couple of hours later I go down to his room where he is watching TV. I open the door and say, "I am leaving for a while….so tomorrow I will take you to get your truck and cell phone. Then you need to go to Enterprise to deal with the damaged car and get your debit card back. Then you need to call the number they gave for an appointment to get some help.   I want you to get on the road to getting things straightened out." He tells me "OK Dad, I understand what needs to be done".

7 days after "That Day"

I start my usual day and prepare to go check on my business. I could hear that Mathew was awake because his TV was on. Through the door, I tell him, "I'm taking off to do my thing. When I get back I will take you to your truck, Ok? A few seconds pass and then I hear an "Ok Dad" from him.

When I return he is dressed and sitting on the porch in his usual chair. He has a magazine that he is looking at and a full backpack next to him. He is ready to get his truck and I am ready to put all of this behind us. I tell him I can take him to his truck now. "I'm just going to stay here and read my magazine" as he pages through 101 Best Cities in the US. I look directly at him, "No we need to get your truck and cell phone like we talked about. You need to go to Enterprise and call that number for counseling". He continues to look at the magazine and doesn't look at me, "No I am just going to stay here and read this magazine." I have had enough of this at this point, "If you refuse to get your truck and do what you need to do, I am calling the police to have you removed from my property". Continuing to page through his magazine he says "Do what you got to do, I am staying right here." I asked him again to get in the car so we can get his truck. Now he just ignores me and pretends I am not there. I call the police with him sitting less than five feet away from me. He just sits there with a stone look on his face. This is no longer my son. This is someone else.

The police arrive. I tell them about the current state of affairs with him. A couple of the officers were at my house the first time. A different sergeant is in charge. I tell him about the mental hospital and that he is refusing to do anything. I tell him that he is scaring me and I want him off my property. In a few minutes, the sergeant comes back and tells me that

Mathew denies he was in a mental hospital. The sergeant felt that he said it in such a convincing way that his experience tells him that he is not ready to seek help. He is denying he has a problem. The police finally convince him he needs to leave. Soon I see the son that I raised and cared about most of my life walking away for good.

8 days after "That Day"

The entire night I am worried that he will come back and try to get in the house. I leave all the outside lights on and hope the dog will wake me up if he tries to come in. At 7:30 in the morning, the doorbell rings. Mathew is standing back from the door just off the porch. His backpack is gone and his pants are visibly soaked almost to his knees. It looks like he had been walking in extremely wet tall grass or in a marshy area. He asked me if he could come in to get some dry socks and his boots. I tell him, "No you are not coming back in the house. Tell me where they are and I will bring them out to you." He responds in a high-pitched voice, "What did I do? Why are you mad at me?" Finally realizing that he was not coming back into the house, he told me where to find his socks and shoes. When I enter his room, I see three large travel bags and his new chainsaw sitting there. It looks like the night before I called the police to have him removed from my property; he packed up a bunch of stuff in preparation to leave. I go outside and give him his dry socks and boots. As he was changing into his dry socks and boots, I brought the bags and chainsaw out and dropped them on the porch. "Get this shit out of here or it will be out to the side of the road in a couple of hours".

About an hour later, I heard the bang of things being loaded into the back of a pickup truck. It was Mathew with his truck loading his crap into the bed. Within five minutes he was gone.

Epilogue

I got one last disjointed hostile text from Mathew and then he blocked me from calling or texting him. His brother Timothy still talks to him I guess. I have told Timothy that unless Mathew can provide me proof that he is in some sort of treatment for his mental illness, I don't want to have anything to do with him. He is living somewhere in the area. I don't want to know where he is or what he is doing. In my mind, unless he gets help, his life will continue to spiral into what will ultimately be a very bad place. I believe that without help he is headed for death or a jail cell. I live in fear every day that I will get a phone call about him. I am afraid he will get his hands on another gun and complete what he tried to do on "that day". I am afraid a delusion will motivate him to do something that will land him in jail. I am afraid his disconnection from reality will cause his death. I am afraid he will come back to hurt me for spoiling his plans.

What I thought was a normal life has now been turned upside down. Decades of money, effort, and caring have suddenly swirled down the drain like a tub full of dirty bath water. Why didn't I recognize what was happening to Mathew? What could I have done differently? Did I spend years enabling him to become what he has become? Was some of this my fault?

I spent decades letting Mathew be Mathew. I was married very young and had my first child when I was 20 years old. My fun years ended abruptly and were replaced by work and the responsibilities of a family. I liked the way Mathew had avoided "growing up" and becoming a responsible adult. I always told his brother that he had more fun in a month than I had at his age in an entire year. I never dreamed that lurking behind the kid who just wanted to avoid responsibilities and have fun was a sleeping mental illness.

I am upset and disheartened that my attempt, to get Mathew the help he needed, through our mental health system, resulted in nothing more than a huge hospital bill. I handed the system a textbook example of a severely mentally ill and dangerous man. The system responded by warehousing him for a few days and then releasing him to the world like he was a stray dog. Now I know why there are mass shootings and all kinds of heinous crimes taking the lives of innocent people across our land. Undiagnosed and untreated people with severe mental illnesses are the invisible demons that live and work among us. They are ticking time bombs whose rage and insanity can ignite at any time and for any reason. And innocent and unsuspecting people become the lambs to their slaughter.

And finally, I hope that what has happened to me and this resulting story will help someone avoid what I have had to go through. I would not wish this on my worst enemy. If you suspect that someone you love has some sort of mental illness, talk to them about it. Encourage them to seek help. Help them in any way you can. Don't wait until it is too late. We sometimes only get one chance to make a difference in someone's life. Don't throw that chance away or let it slip through your fingers. You must always try to do the right thing even if it goes horribly wrong.

www.ingramcontent.com/pod-product-compliance
Lightning Source LLC
Chambersburg PA
CBHW061025250726
48662CB00011B/2133